COVERED BRIDGES

Joseph D. Conwill

Published in Great Britain in 2014 by Shire Publications Ltd, PO Box 883, Oxford, OX1 9PL, UK.

PO Box 3985, New York, NY 10185-3985, USA.

E-mail: shire@shirebooks.co.uk
www.shirebooks.co.uk

A CIP catalogue record for this book is available from the British Library.

Shire Library no. 808.   ISBN-13: 978 0 74781 449 8
PDF e-book ISBN: 978 1 78442 011 6
ePub ISBN: 978 1 78442 010 9

Joseph D. Conwill has asserted his right under the Copyright, Designs and Patents Act, 1988, to be identified as the author of this book.

Designed by Tony Truscott Designs, Sussex, UK and typeset in Garamond Pro and Gill Sans.

Printed in China through Worldprint Ltd.

14 15 16 17 18   10 9 8 7 6 5 4 3 2 1

COVER IMAGE
The covered bridge at West Arlington, Vermont, New England. (Alamy)

TITLE PAGE IMAGE
Hamden Bridge in Delaware County, New York is shown in this 1972 photograph. Part of the old structure still stands, but it has been heavily reworked.

CONTENTS PAGE IMAGE
Geiger's Bridge graces the Jordan Creek valley northwest of Allentown. It has the false-front portals sometimes found on covered bridges of southeastern Pennsylvania. The stone parapets along the approaches are typical of the region.

ACKNOWLEDGMENTS
Acknowledgments to follow

IMAGE ACKNOWLEDGMENTS
Most of the photographs in this book were taken by the author himself from 1966 to 2013. The following images are from the archives of the National Society for the Preservation of Covered Bridges: page 6, by Carl Cranmer; page 19; page 20; pages 24–25, by Richard Sanders Allen; page 36 (top) by Richard Sanders Allen; page 37; page 40, by Richard Sanders Allen.

Shire Publications is supporting the Woodland Trust, the UK's leading woodland conservation charity, by funding the dedication of trees.

CONTENTS

INTRODUCTION

THE OLD COVERED bridge is a powerful symbol of American rural life. The timber tunnel, fragrant and mysterious, carries the traveler safely over a gurgling stream, along the road from bright green fields to cool shady woods. This dreamworld image does not always match reality, but it comes close often enough to make covered bridges among the most popular symbols of Americana. They are also very accessible symbols, being found in most parts of the United States except for the High Plains and the Rockies, and in much of eastern Canada as well.

The redevelopment of the rural economy as a suburban one, based on travel to jobs elsewhere, has made covered bridge preservation more difficult. Most covered bridges as originally built could have carried heavy loads such as school buses, fire engines, or oil trucks on an occasional basis, but the bridges suffered from decades of neglect which weakened many of them early in the twentieth century. Until the 1960s the common expectation was that the covered bridges would eventually all be replaced with concrete, and many did not receive even routine maintenance. Since then, their popularity has inspired various efforts to keep them in service, although the vastly increased traffic volume on rural roads brings special challenges in dealing with one-lane bridges. Bypassing them is a possibility, but all structures need repairs now and then, and it is often hard to find funding for repairs unless the bridge is still carrying traffic.

Opposite: This lovely covered bridge in the Gatineau Valley of Québec is just a few miles north of Canada's capital city of Ottawa, Ontario.

The historical period of covered bridge construction lasted from about 1805 to 1955. In the northeastern United States no new covered bridges were built after World War I. Construction in the Midwest lasted into the 1920s, and in parts of the South into the 1930s. In the Pacific Northwest, and also in parts of eastern Canada, where large supplies of high quality timber were still locally available, covered bridge construction lasted into the 1950s. The later

covered bridges were built for automobile traffic from the very start. The United States still has 674 covered bridges from this historical time period, although over a third of them have been significantly modernized. Canada has 144, and more of them are original because on average they are more recent.

The popularity of the covered bridge concept inspired several thousand imitations from the mid-1950s onwards. Most of these were mere decorative shells erected over concrete bridges, or structures built of small dimension lumber in backyards. They obviously had no relation to the historical prototypes other than as testaments to their popularity, but guidebooks and press accounts often cited them as if they were real. This explains the wild misstatements still frequently encountered that there are over eight hundred, or fifteen hundred, or even three thousand covered bridges in the United States, for by now the modern imitations greatly outnumber the originals, just as recent suburban houses of "colonial" style outnumber real colonial-era dwellings.

From the late 1960s onwards, a greater awareness of historical building techniques led to the construction of a few new covered bridges that closely resembled the old ones. At first they were all-new road crossings, or else replacements for old covered bridges that had been accidentally lost to floods or fire. Their widespread acceptance in the historical world, however, allowed an unfortunate new phase of history starting in the 1980s: a number of old covered bridges have now been intentionally torn down and replaced with replicas. Most of these bridges could have been strengthened by the addition of laminated arches, a common reinforcement technique in the late-nineteenth century, but now they are completely lost. Even very good replicas lack the real physical connection with the past of structures "washed by the passing waves of humanity," in Ruskin's famous phrase. Covered bridges are our only

Opposite: The former Columbia–Portland Bridge over the Delaware River between New Jersey and Pennsylvania shows the mystery of the long, timbered tunnel. It was an excellent example of the Burr truss type of construction.

historical monuments for which modern reproductions are widely offered as equivalent to the originals, and their future is far from secure, despite their popularity.

A covered bridge is a truss bridge, a complicated framework built up of relatively short pieces of timber, which can carry loads across spans much longer than the individual timbers themselves. Americans used wood because it was inexpensive and widely available, but by the 1790s it was obvious that unprotected wooden structures had short life spans, often just ten or fifteen years. Wood preservatives did not yet exist; paint was sometimes used, but water could still infiltrate cracks and joints. Builders in central Europe also used timber, and from late-medieval times onwards they had roofed their bridges to prevent decay. A few Swiss examples were widely publicized in America from the late 1700s onwards by travelers and technical writers. China also built large numbers of covered wooden bridges, but these were completely unknown in the West until very recently.

By 1800 Americans too were discussing covered bridges. The idea was in the air, but it seems not to have been imported directly from Europe despite some knowledge of the precedent. American bridge builders did not adopt the heavy-timbered arch-brace designs that were popular in Switzerland, nor was there any cross-Atlantic interchange of talent, as happened for example in the history of military fortifications.

Timothy Palmer's "Permanent Bridge" over the Schuylkill River at Philadelphia, completed in 1805, was the first known American covered bridge. Palmer (1751–1821) was a long-established builder of open wooden bridges over major rivers such as the Merrimack and the Piscataqua, and the Permanent Bridge came near the end of his career. He covered it at the suggestion of a major investor in the toll bridge company that owned it, and the idea immediately proved its worth. Philadelphia's Permanent Bridge lasted

Opposite: Suvorov Bridge graces the alpine landscape of Canton Schwyz in Switzerland. American designers knew of a few Swiss bridges, but they did not copy Swiss styles of building.

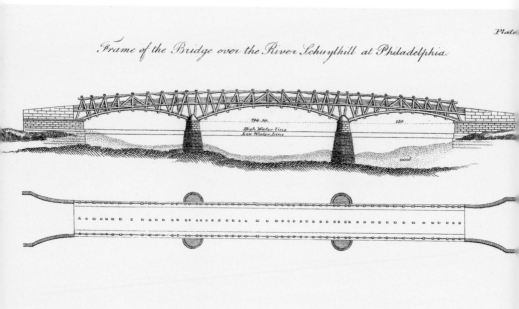

Frame of the Bridge over the River Schuylkill at Philadelphia.

Timothy Palmer's Permanent Bridge at Philadelphia combined arch and truss forms. This drawing is from Thomas Pope's 1811 *Treatise on Bridge Architecture.*

forty-five years, and was torn down in 1850 only because a new bridge for a railroad was needed on the site. Within just a few years of its construction, covered bridges became the standard for important river crossings.

These earliest covered bridges were grandiose affairs. They served major traffic arteries, often in or near cities, so they were two lanes wide. They were also very expensive. Palmer's Permanent Bridge cost over $275,000, an enormous sum in 1805. However, they were highly visible public examples, and the idea of covering timber bridges to protect them from decay soon spread even to lesser river crossings and quieter places. By 1830 the covered bridge was a standard structure everywhere, not just on important roads. The later examples were usually smaller, plainer, and one lane wide. They were much less expensive, too. Throughout the nineteenth century, a covered bridge of a generous 150-foot span might cost $5,000 including the foundations; short ones on existing foundations could even cost less than $1,000.

THE BUILDING OF A BRIDGE

THE VERY EARLIEST covered bridges were built by private capital. Governments then did not have sufficient tax revenue to fund major public works; as a result they chartered corporations, which they closely regulated. When covered bridges later became the standard even for modest crossings of country streams, local governments were able to build them—usually those of the towns in the Northeast, or of the counties in other parts of the United States. Citizens who saw the need for a new bridge would bring the matter before Town Meeting or petition the county commissioners; if approved, officials would solicit bids for the project. If it involved an all-new crossing, there would usually be separate bids for the stonework foundations and for the timber bridge itself; the stonework could amount to half of the cost of the project. Many projects involved replacement of previous structures lost to flood or accident, and there the old foundations could often be re-used.

These foundations included an abutment on either riverbank. If the distance between them was too long for a one-span timber truss, there would be piers in the river as well. Foundation styles varied widely by the region. Dry-laid masonry, using split but unfinished stone, was the usual choice in New England. Eastern Pennsylvania used random mortared masonry, including a wing wall along the approach, which rose high enough to form a guard rail known as a parapet. Western Pennsylvania

Shinn Bridge in Washington County, Ohio sits on well-made, cut-stone abutments. Cut stone was widely used from western Pennsylvania through Illinois.

and the Midwest favored cut and finished masonry. The South used various kinds of stone, although Mississippi sometimes used brick. Everywhere timber bents were occasionally substituted, either for lower cost or because the stream banks were not stable enough to emplace stone; in the western Midwest these were sometimes replaced with steel tubes. Covered bridges in eastern Canada often sat on timber cribs filled with loose stone. In Oregon, where covered bridges were built into the 1950s, the abutments were usually concrete.

When the foundations were done, the timber framers went to work. They usually laid out the trusses first in a field nearby, or sometimes at a work yard near home, to make the cuts and to be sure everything fitted precisely. Then they disassembled the work and put it back together on location, on staging known as "falsework" over the river. Once the bridge was ready for service, the falsework was knocked away. Sometimes the builders waited until later to add the roofing and side boarding.

Builders used a wide variety of timber species depending on what was available, either locally, or on the market. The South usually used its local yellow pine. The Northeast often used white pine in the early days, but in later times used spruce, which has a high ratio of strength to weight. The Midwest sometimes used Michigan white pine while it was still available, but also locally cut species such as poplar, and occasionally in later years yellow pine imported from the South. White oak and various other hardwoods also found use in the Midwest; however, they are heavy, and the biggest load a timber bridge has to carry is its own weight. Oregon of course used its magnificent Douglas fir. Spruce found wide application in eastern Canada. Everywhere, other species found specific uses; for example, oak was used for treenails (pronounced trunnels), the pins which held joints together.

This covered bridge at Île Nepawa in far-western Québec uses timber cribs for abutments. If the cribs decay, they can be replaced without tearing down the entire bridge.

TRADITIONAL TIMBER FRAMING

STUDENTS OF FRAMING history identify a change in method that took place in the years before 1830. In the earlier method, known as the scribe rule, every piece was custom cut to the place it was to occupy. In the later method, the square rule, builders struck a reference line to which every piece conformed, so that pieces were interchangeable. This distinction is easy to document in residential or barn framing, but it applies only imperfectly to bridges. Architects did invent some types of bridge framing that called for standard parts; however, some of the older truss types required all custom work anyway, and these continued in use into the twentieth century alongside the supposedly more modern forms. Although bridge framing required many of the same tools and skills as house or barn work, it is a very different task from an engineering point of view to produce a long structure held up only at the ends, rather than a framework which is supported on foundations at every point all around.

Barns, churches, and other large structures did however require some bridge-building skills to hold up the roof. Kingpost and queenpost trusses had long been used for this purpose, and they carried over naturally to bridge building, along with an extended form known as the multiple kingpost truss.

Covered bridge trusses may be divided into two types: those which required a large amount of traditional notched joinery, and those which minimized this labor. Traditional

Opposite:
Sunday River
Bridge in Newry,
Maine shows
the elongated
counter ties that
are characteristic
of the Paddleford
truss.

McLeary Brook Bridge in Carleton County, New Brunswick is a kingpost truss in its late form, using a metal rod instead of a wooden post in the middle. Kingpost trusses had short spans, and many of them were never covered.

framers used a variety of joints depending on the kind of stress that needed to be carried. The top horizontal piece of a bridge is called the top chord; on the bottom is the bottom chord. Posts could be joined to the top chord with a mortise and tenon, a projection on the top of the post

William Mitten Bridge in Albert County, New Brunswick has carpenter's match marks to ensure that every piece went in the right place. Such marks are rarely visible in covered bridges, although they are common in barn framing.

Fowlersville Bridge in Columbia County, Pennsylvania is an excellent example of the queenpost truss in its most basic form. Longer bridges sometimes used extra timbers in the middle.

which fits into a pocket cut into the chord, pinned with treenails. Such a joint is not strong enough for the bottom chord, which carries the weight of the floor. The most common post-bottom chord joint required a two-part chord, through which the posts passed, notched into both faces. A short extra length of post protruded below the chord to prevent shearing of the timber from undoing

Dingleton Bridge in Cornish, New Hampshire, is a multiple kingpost truss. This simple truss uses a series of vertical posts, with diagonal braces all inclined towards the center.

A close look at the joinery details of the Scott Bridge near Jeffersonville, Vermont reveals the large amount of skilled custom labor needed to build it.

the joint. Sometimes this two-part chord was used on top as well. Diagonal braces could be secured by cutting shoulders on the posts in a variety of ways. All this work required much labor, and it had to be done very precisely if the bridge was to last without sagging.

Timothy Palmer, builder of America's first known covered bridge in 1805, used traditional timber joinery. His entire bridge frame was arched, both the top and bottom chords. Between the arches, forming the walls of the bridge, he used multiple kingpost trussing with the posts flared; that is, they inclined outwards towards the ends of the bridge, approximately perpendicular to the arch. The bridge floor was arched too. In such a design every piece was different, and the entire structure had to be custom cut. It was expensive work, but it produced a strong bridge. Although a few other early builders used his truss, it never gained a specific regional following, and no examples exist today.

Theodore Burr (1771–1822) was a somewhat younger man, and during his career he built mostly covered bridges.

He experimented widely, and eventually settled on a form that, like Palmer's, used an arch, but combined with the trusswork in a different manner. The Burr truss, patented in 1817, was a multiple-kingpost design with level top and bottom chords, to which a separate arch was bolted, usually on both sides. In his design the floor of the bridge was level. The Burr truss was labor-intensive; however, in his patent specifications Burr recommended simplifying the work by mitering the braces into the corners formed by the post-chord joint, instead of cutting a notch or shoulder on the post. So far as we know he did not follow this advice himself. The few interior photographs of bridges built by Burr show the braces framed into the posts in the old traditional way.

The Burr truss proved very popular in the building tradition. Just under two hundred still exist, making it the most common form of covered bridge construction. Prominently located early examples of a bridge type influenced the later distribution of a design, and the Burr

The former Deer Island Bridge west of Newburyport, Massachusetts shows the arched shape of Timothy Palmer's bridges.

truss was widely used from the start. It is found today in northern Vermont, and in nearly all of Pennsylvania, the Midwest, and the upper South. An unusual variant form was also used in the province of New Brunswick, Canada.

Lieutenant-Colonel Stephen H. Long (1784–1864) patented a bridge truss in 1830 that also made extensive use of traditional timber joinery, but which incorporated new and sophisticated engineering concepts. Long was a man of diverse talents, and was famous as a Western explorer. His engineering work involved early railroading, where very strong bridges were needed. The Long truss used a series of boxed Xs with counterbrace wedges inserted at strategic points to allow prestressing of the truss so that it would not deflect under load. Although it was used for highways as well as for railroads, many later builders did not fully understand the concept, and omitted the special wedges. The Long truss produced a strong bridge, but it required diligent maintenance, and was complicated to build. It soon fell out of favor when other good designs appeared that required less labor in construction. Less than a dozen examples remain, scattered sparsely from Maine through West Virginia and Indiana.

During the 1830s Peter Paddleford (1785–1859) developed a final entry in the field of traditionally built bridge trusses. His design started with a multiple-kingpost frame, with braces in compression, but he also added counter ties in the other direction, functioning in tension. The ties are notched intricately through the chords, and they overlap the posts, producing a design that is visually distinctive. Paddleford did not patent his truss, but it gained an important regional following in his home territory of northern New England, where twenty-one examples still stand.

Robyville Bridge northwest of Bangor, Maine is an excellent example of the Long truss, and is very close to the style of the original patent.

LABOR-SAVING BRIDGE DESIGNS

A MERICA WAS ALWAYS short of labor in the early nineteenth century. The same cultural pressures that brought simplified square-rule framing to the work yard also inspired some entirely new bridge truss designs to reduce traditional timber-framing labor.

The first of these, the Town lattice truss, was patented in 1820 by prominent architect Ithiel Town (1784–1844). It resembled a heavily built garden trellis, and had no vertical posts. The Town lattice truss was built of standard sawn planks, often three by ten inches, pinned together where they overlapped with very large treenails. Although labor was needed to bore the holes for these treenails, which had to be plumb and precisely sized, there were no mortise-and-tenon connections or other complicated joinery. Early prototypes of the truss tended to warp, but Town solved the problem by adding extra chords for greater stiffness.

Ithiel Town was a native of Connecticut, but his architectural practice extended up and down the Eastern Seaboard; he was working on a commission in North Carolina when he patented his bridge truss. Early prototypes there resulted in the Town lattice truss becoming the dominant form for covered bridges from the Carolinas through Mississippi. Isaac Damon, one of Town's business partners, did a good job introducing it to New England, where it is found today from central New Hampshire through much of Vermont, and also across New York State. New Englanders brought the idea to the

Opposite:
North Pole
Bridge in Brown
County, Ohio
is a Smith truss,
one of the later
styles of timber
truss design.

Although the former Shedd's Bridge near Walloomsac, New York was sadly neglected in its later years, it was possible to see its Town lattice truss very clearly.

Western Reserve of northeastern Ohio, which today is still Town lattice territory. The province of Québec is too. The 187 existing historical Town lattice trusses make this form a close second to the Burr truss for popularity in North America.

William Howe (1803–52) invented another very popular labor-saving bridge truss, on which he received a series of patents from 1840 through to 1846. The early patents covered some experimental designs, but the final form that he had developed by the mid-1840s was a series

of boxed Xs looking much like the Long truss. Instead of wooden posts and adjustment wedges, however, the Howe truss used vertical iron rods, which could be tightened firmly with bolts. It could easily be adjusted later even if built with unseasoned lumber, a big advantage in a nation where railroads in particular were beginning to need large numbers of strong bridges in a hurry. The braces were seated on special angle blocks, so the bridge required no intricate, traditionally framed joints. Parts for Howe trusses were sometimes precut by large bridge-building companies, and

This non-covered bridge over Fraser River near Yellowhead Pass in British Columbia gives a clear idea of the Howe truss, often used elsewhere for covered bridges.

sent out for erection on site like kits; local contractors, however, often cut their own parts, ordering only the iron hardware from away.

The Howe truss became popular for highway use too, yet despite its obvious advantages, its following was not universal. Conservative New Englanders kept to their Burr, Paddleford, or Town lattice trusses, while most of Pennsylvania continued to build Burr trusses, and much of the South still used the Town lattice. The Howe truss did find favor from Ohio across the Midwest, but it had to compete with the Burr truss even there. Only on the West Coast and in New Brunswick did the Howe truss become the dominant form. North America today has 161 historical examples, making this covered bridge truss the third most popular. The Howe truss also found a regional following as a non-covered timber truss, after chemical wood preservatives became widely available.

The last major entry in the field of labor-saving timber trusses was the work of Robert W. Smith (1833–98). The Smith truss, patented in 1867, used carefully notched timbers, and at first glance it seems like an older traditional design. However, the precision cuts were all made at the central factory of the Smith Bridge Company, in Ohio, or its affiliate the Pacific Bridge Company, in California. The precut parts were shipped by rail or barge wherever Smith's sales agents could sell bridges, and local contractors assembled them. It was possible for local people to buy plans and cut the parts themselves, but this practice was less common. When Robert Smith received his patent, iron was just coming into wide use as a bridge-building material; wood, however, still had a cost advantage, and his truss was designed to use it as efficiently as possible. Most of the twenty-three remaining Smith trusses are in Ohio and Indiana.

Cataract Falls Bridge in Owen County, Indiana is a fine example of the Smith truss. The parts for Smith trusses were usually fabricated at the Smith Bridge Company factory in Ohio.

TWENTIETH-CENTURY COVERED BRIDGES

THREE REGIONS OF North America continued to build covered bridges into the 1950s: Oregon, Québec, and New Brunswick. Inexpensive, locally available, high-quality construction timber allowed covered bridges to remain cost-effective in all three regions.

Oregon favored the modern Howe truss from the start. A. S. Miller, a Smith Bridge Company affiliate, also built many Smith trusses; although the style remained popular for a while in southern Oregon even after the patent ran out, none remain in the state today. The steel shortage of World War I, coupled with some unhappy experiences with flimsily built metal bridges, encouraged Oregon to take another look at its rich timber reserves as the solution to its bridge problems.

The State Highway Commission drew up standard plans for covered bridges, and made them available to the county engineers. Primary responsibility for most bridges rested with the county. These local engineers prepared their own plans, based on the state standards for loading, but using their own inspiration for the finer construction details and for the housing. Even more interesting was the adaption of the modern Howe truss to the richness of the timber materials available. Although the Howe truss could be built like a kit and shipped in from afar, local transportation was a problem; since good timber was standing nearly everywhere, it made more sense to cut and frame the timbers on or near the site. The truss

Opposite: Bolduc Bridge near Sainte-Clotilde is a good example of the Québec "colonization bridge." It was still painted the original red color when this view was captured in 1975.

used angle blocks to eliminate complicated joinery, but if a crew was already working with hand tools to shape the timbers, it did not require much extra work to cut notches to receive the braces in the old-time timber-framing style, instead of using blocks. Steel rods were brought in from away, but otherwise this modern truss was often adapted to remote near-frontier conditions, and ended up being built with work methods much like those of a century earlier. Construction lasted into the early 1950s, and died out only when concrete and steel became so widely available that they gained the cost advantage, while increasing labor costs made timber bridges more expensive.

Earnest Bridge, dating from 1938, is typical of the twentieth-century covered bridges of Lane County, Oregon.

Québec built covered bridges throughout the nineteenth century, generally using the North American bridge patrimony—multiple kingpost, Burr, Town lattice, and Howe trusses. The province entered a new and distinctive phase of covered bridge history when Premier Honoré Mercier created the Department of Colonization in 1887. Québec at the time was vigorously expanding its agricultural frontiers. Land-settlement projects were usually organized by the Catholic Church, and the new department offered services such as road and bridge construction. It soon became evident that covered wooden bridges, built by the new settlers themselves, would provide the most cost-effective river crossings.

A close look up into the timbers of the 1925 Currin Bridge of Lane County, Oregon shows that the brace (at left) was mill-sawn, but the top chord piece was hand-hewn, because the big stick was too long for a sawmill carriage.

The Town lattice truss was already well known in Québec, but the Department of Colonization modified it to permit construction by unskilled labor. Since the truss used sawn planks, the old timber framing methods were not required. Instead of treenails, the "colonization bridges" used metal spikes at the joints. Their lattice web was made of smaller lumber than was usual elsewhere. To add strength and stability, the department added vertical posts every eight feet, a modification also found in a few earlier bridges in the province. Colonization bridges went up by the hundreds in the far-flung, newly settled lands of Abitibi, Lac-Saint-Jean, and the Gaspé Peninsula. The Department of Colonization was also involved in expanding the limits of the long-settled parishes in Québec's older heartland, and the special bridges are still found today in every part of the province. Once painted red, and therefore known as *ponts rouges,* the province began repainting them gray with green trim after World War II; today they come in a variety of colors. The most recent were built in the mid-1950s.

Neighboring New Brunswick was the very last bastion of historical covered bridge construction, one having been built in 1958. The early history of covered bridges in the province is little known. Here the Howe truss was always popular, but New Brunswick also developed its own special version of the Burr truss. It used flared posts, the panel size (that is, the space between the posts) diminished towards the ends of the bridge. Instead of a true arch, it used straight braces covering about the last third of the bridge at each end, earning it the local name "strutted Burr truss." Another variety had a true arch rising up over the top chord, but was apparently built only as a non-covered timber truss. For although New Brunswick did build many covered bridges, the province also used non-covered timber trusses treated with creosote.

The former Gardner Creek Bridge, on the Bay of Fundy shore in Saint John County, was typical of New Brunswick's many covered bridges.

British Columbia did not build covered bridges, but it did build non-covered creosoted timber trusses, nearly all of the Howe design. Although creosote does not protect wood as well as a roof and sides, some of the British Columbia examples have served up to eighty years. They do not have a popular following such as covered bridges do elsewhere, but they are part of the same line of engineering history.

This non-housed timber bridge near Temperance Vale shows the form of New Brunswick's unusual variant Burr truss, also once widely used for covered bridges in the province.

The covered bridges of the twentieth century were designed by trained professional engineers, who one might suppose would have created some new and perhaps more scientific way of doing things. But the nineteenth-century inventors had already given much careful consideration to the most efficient ways to build strong wooden bridges. Twentieth-century engineers brought more attention to issues such as correct sizing of timbers to the loads they had to carry, but the basic designs they used were the ones already proven by the 1840s: the Burr, the Town lattice, and the Howe.

THE CHALLENGE OF PRESERVATION

T HE COVERED BRIDGE era began drawing to a close in the Northeast in the 1890s. Popular opinion viewed the old bridges as eyesores, dark and smelly inside, which attracted vagrants and hooligans, and should be replaced with something modern as soon as possible. Such an attitude meant the death of many a covered bridge that was still structurally sound. Yet even then a few rare individuals saw something special in the bridges, and began to photograph them as they were disappearing. By the 1920s postcard producers featured covered bridges among their offerings, notably the Eastern Illustrating and Publishing Company of Belfast, Maine.

Before 1930 the published literature on covered bridges was restricted to old technical materials from the nineteenth century, but the broadening public interest in the subject brought new titles to print, written from a historical or at least an antiquarian perspective. Rosalie Wells's *Covered Bridges in America* (1931) was one of the first. Artist Eric Sloane's widely circulated *American Barns and Covered Bridges* (1954) brought even more attention to the subject. However, the early books were steeped in myth and contained little solid historical research. Public misconceptions still abounded, for example that covered bridges dated from colonial times, or that George Washington had crossed this one or that. Even the reason for covering bridges—to protect the trusswork from decay—was forgotten.

Opposite:
The 1889 Paper Mill Bridge in Bennington, Vermont, seen in this 1966 photo, was torn down and replaced with an all-new covered bridge in 2000.

Bridges neglected as badly as this central Pennsylvania specimen eventually develop serious decay that is very complicated to correct later.

Richard Sanders Allen (1917–2008) brought precision to the subject. Allen first became interested in covered bridges at the age of twenty, and he spent much of his life doing meticulous historical research. His regional historical books, starting with *Covered Bridges of the Northeast* (1957; many later editions) are still important references on the subject. Allen was a remarkable person with a photographic memory, an analytical mind, and boundless enthusiasm for any subject that he researched. He found a sympathetic publisher in the Stephen Greene Press of Brattleboro,

Big Run Bridge in Noble County, Ohio had passed the point of no return when this photograph was taken in 1976.

Vermont, which made a specialty of covered bridge books until Greene's untimely death in an airplane crash in the 1970s. Allen founded the magazine *Covered Bridge Topics* in 1943, and it is still published today.

Before 1960 even those who thought preserving covered bridges was worthwhile accepted the idea that most of them would eventually be lost. They focused their attention on saving a significant few. Vrest Orton, noted ruralist and chairman of the Vermont Historic Sites Commission, worked on recommendations for preserving one covered bridge for each of the state's counties. Moving bridges to museums was another possibility. The Henry Ford Museum's Greenfield Village moved a Pennsylvania covered bridge to its collection of Americana in 1937. The Shelburne Museum saved a Vermont covered bridge in 1951 by moving it partway across the state, and the following year Old Sturbridge Village relocated another Vermont covered bridge to its museum in central Massachusetts. Orton himself saved a Vermont bridge in 1967 by moving it to his country store in Rockingham.

Historian Richard Sanders Allen was sometimes known as "Mr. Covered Bridge," although he was a respected authority on other subjects as well.

Engineers in the 1950s received little or no training in the use of timber, and they distrusted it. One honorable exception was Roy Wentzel (1894–1985), chief of bridge maintenance for the Maine Highway Commission. He convinced the state to take over responsibility for all of Maine's covered bridges, since the state had better financial resources than the towns that formerly owned most of them. He then proceeded to restore them, and his successors at what is now the Department of Transportation have shared his fondness for the bridges. Many of them are now bypassed, but they are kept in repair. Maine had ten covered bridges in 1960. Although three were later lost to arson or flood, two of these have been rebuilt as covered bridges.

Hemlock Bridge over the Old Channel of the Saco River in Fryeburg, Maine, is an example of the bridges saved through the interest of state engineer Roy Wentzel.

The task of preservation was perhaps easier here than elsewhere, because Maine had relatively few structures to look after. Most of them would surely be gone by now had it not been for Roy Wentzel's skills and the public example he set that covered bridge preservation is possible.

By the late 1960s popular interest in covered bridges had grown to the point that preservation of all of them was at last seriously considered. In some cases when bridges could no longer carry heavy loads, their original floors were cut out and replaced with hidden steel beams. A few covered bridges were modified in this way as far back as the 1930s, but by the 1970s it became almost a standard treatment. As one tourist remarked when looking underneath a southeastern Pennsylvania bridge, "That's cheating!" Much of the variety of historical floor framing has now been lost. Not everyone agreed that steel reinforcement was the answer, though. One prominent critic was Milton Graton (1908–94) of Ashland, New Hampshire, who began repairing covered bridges in the 1950s using traditional timber-framing skills that had largely been forgotten.

The Cornish–Windsor Bridge over the Connecticut River between New Hampshire and Vermont is the longest historical covered bridge in the United States, at 460 feet. It needed reinforcement in the 1980s, and the job became a battleground between those advocating traditional techniques and those who wanted to use modern materials. Milton Graton prepared a proposal for the traditionalists, who were ably led by David W. Wright (1940–2013) of nearby Westminster, Vermont.

Bridgewright Milton Graton was a prominent spokesman for traditional covered bridge repair. This photograph shows him on the job in New Hampshire in 1983.

His plan called for the addition of laminated arches, which is how a bridge would have been strengthened in the nineteenth century. Here, however, the arches would have changed the exterior appearance of the bridge. The modernists proposed instead to cut out the bottom of the historical trusswork and replace the bottom chords entirely with glue-laminated material. Much of the original structure would be lost, although the bridge would keep the same familiar outward look.

The modernists won the Cornish–Windsor battle, and the job has set an unfortunate precedent for repair work since then. However, all was not lost for the traditionalists. David W. Wright went on to become president of the National Society for the Preservation of Covered Bridges, or NSPCB. This group had been founded in 1950, and made a mark early on in the preservation world, advocating for covered bridges. From the 1960s through the 1980s, however, the NSPCB lost its way, when the more prominent members developed a strong interest in tracking down recently built backyard imitation covered bridges, instead of the true historical ones. Wright put the group mostly back on track, and the NSPCB is today in the forefront of the movement for traditional bridge repair. Meanwhile the Historic American Engineering Record (HAER), a branch

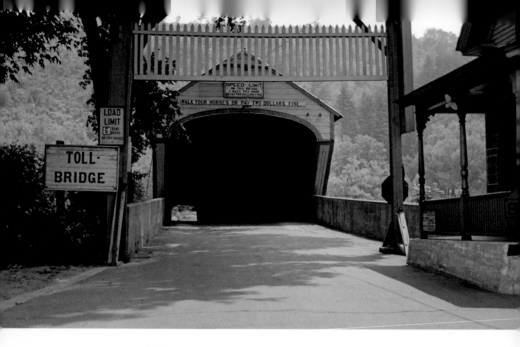

Crossing the Cornish–Windsor Bridge required paying a toll when Richard Sanders Allen took this photograph around 1940. The bridge was the focus of an important preservation dispute in the late 1980s.

of the National Park Service, has been doing a thorough job of documenting the bridges with historical research, photographs, and engineering studies.

Covered bridges need a voice now more than ever. A number of high-quality earlier restorations have recently been redone, not because of quality problems, but because local officials later decided that even higher load limits were needed. Skilled and sensitive engineers and timber framers are now working in the field, but much work is still done by generalists without a strong foundation in historic preservation. Local framing variations are too little respected; several covered bridges have emerged from major work well capable of carrying modern loads, but redesigned to some generic plan that makes them much less interesting as historical monuments. Portals and sides are often redone in a cumbersome style that does not match the original, and a few have even received phony barn doors or cutesy cupolas.

The painstaking work of tracking down all of the damage in a long-neglected bridge sometimes leads to a decision to tear it down completely and replace it with a copy.

The National Register of Historic Places is supposed to contain only old historical structures; however, the listings are mainly updated by state and local officials, who sometimes neglect this task. When an old covered bridge is replaced with an entirely new copy, but the Register continues to list it with the original construction date, the impression received is that outward appearance is the important issue, not historical integrity. Traditionalists then face the accusation of being out-of-touch "purists," and the prestige of the Register itself is used unintentionally to support the removal of historical structures. Even the National Society for the Preservation of Covered Bridges recognizes bridges as authentic if they are built like the old ones, regardless of when they were really constructed, which unwittingly removes the reason for saving the originals. Covered bridges are not friendless, but they need more friends with a real appreciation of history.

The burnt remains of the Emmetsville Bridge in Randolph County, Indiana remained standing for several months after an arson attack in 1973.

Arson—fire for the fun of it—has been another major threat to covered bridges for more than a half-century. Since 1952 the United States has lost at least 170 covered bridges to arson, and Canada another sixty-six. On occasion the fires are set by disgruntled local residents who want a new bridge, but most often it is just for kicks. Remote bridges that have become the scene of regular nocturnal parties are a prime target. Every part of North America has lost covered bridges to arson, excepting the West Coast where, for cultural reasons that have not yet been investigated, the problem is almost unknown.

COVERED BRIDGES TODAY, REGION BY REGION

VERMONT

Vermont is said to have one hundred covered bridges, but the figure needs a closer look. Eighty-five of these do in fact date from the historical time period, although the amount of original timber varies much from bridge to bridge. Twelve are modern total replacements of old covered bridges, while three are recent covered bridges on new sites.

Southwestern Vermont has an 1852-vintage covered bridge at West Arlington near a traditional New England church. Brown Bridge, deep in the woods in Shrewsbury near Rutland, is also of special interest. Rutland County was a historical center of the slate industry, and Brown Bridge has a slate roof dating from its original construction in 1880. Builder Nichols Powers made skillful use of a large streamside boulder for one of the abutments.

Addison County has a "double-barrel," or two-lane, covered bridge near downtown Middlebury. Another more modest bridge northeast of the town once sat on some of the tallest dry-laid stone abutments ever built. A rare covered railroad bridge stands on an abandoned branch of the Rutland Railroad near East Shoreham.

In southeastern Vermont, Willard's Bridge at North Hartland enjoys an interesting site near a large waterfall, improbably wedged between Interstate 91 and a railroad line that still sees daily passenger service. It spans the north channel of the Ottauquechee River to a small rocky island,

Opposite: Knight's Ferry Bridge evokes the old-time West in Stanislaus County, California. It is now bypassed, but when this photograph was taken in 1978 it was still in use, with traffic lights to regulate passage through the one-lane bridge.

The south end of the Brown Bridge in Shrewsbury, Vermont rested on a large boulder, very slightly filled out with dry-laid stone. The boulder still remains, although the bridge has been raised, and a little more masonry has been added since this photo was taken in 1973.

on the south side of which is a new covered bridge built in 2001 by timber framer Jan Lewandoski. Taftsville Bridge, also over the Ottauquechee, dates from 1836 and is among the oldest covered bridges in the nation.

This archival photograph shows the top of one of the tall, dry-laid stone abutments that once held up the Halpin Bridge of Middlebury, Vermont. Although the bridge still stands, today's visitor will find concrete abutments instead.

In central Vermont, the upper branches of the White River are rich in covered bridges, all set in very attractive hill farm landscapes. Northfield Falls is also a covered bridge haven, having four covered bridges very near each other.

Shoreham Railroad Bridge is now surrounded by woods. It is kept in good repair, but this 1966 photograph cannot be retaken.

A view from the Moxley Bridge in Chelsea shows the lovely countryside of central Vermont. This bridge is in close to original condition, as are most of the others in the valley of the First Branch of the White River.

Mill Bridge stood in the village of Tunbridge, Vermont. It was removed by burning when a major flood threatened to dislodge it and take out other bridges downstream. Today a copy built in 2000 stands on the site.

Northern Vermont is prime covered bridge territory too. Fisher Bridge in Wolcott is another rare covered railroad bridge, no longer used, but preserved in a park next to busy Route 15. Cambridge once had a double-barrel covered bridge right on this highway, but it was moved to the

Tunbridge, Vermont is also home to the Flint Bridge, seen in this 1940s view by Richard Sanders Allen.

Shelburne Museum in 1951. Montgomery was still home to six covered bridges at the end of the twentieth century, with a seventh just over the town line in Enosburg. Their condition gradually deteriorated, and their complete restoration was beyond the means of this small town. With state aid, four have been renovated; one has been torn down and replaced with a modern copy, while a second awaits the same fate; and one has been taken apart and placed in storage.

NEW HAMPSHIRE AND MAINE

New Hampshire has forty-five historical covered bridges, plus seven modern ones of a style resembling the old. Most of the new bridges have replaced old ones lost to arson, or are at sites that did not have covered bridges before. Three of New Hampshire's covered bridges are shared with Vermont, crossing the Connecticut River: the Cornish–Windsor

The covered bridge of Stark, New Hampshire enjoys a setting next to a church, with an impressive cliff in the background.

The rare pony truss railroad bridge in Randolph, New Hampshire was still in service when this photograph was taken in 1985.

Bridge, plus two others further north. Columbia Bridge, between Columbia, New Hampshire, and Lemington, Vermont, was built in 1912 and was the last old covered bridge built on a New England public road.

Coös County, in the state's northern tip, has one of the most photographed covered bridges in the United States at Stark. It is a Paddleford truss with the graceful arched portal and deeply overhanging eaves that often accompany this truss style. Another area attraction, but much less known, is an abandoned pony truss railroad bridge crossing Snyder Brook in Randolph. Pony trusses are timber bridges with low sides boarded in separately, without a roof overhead. They are closely related to covered bridges historically, but they lacked popular appeal, and have almost completely disappeared.

Bath–Haverhill Bridge over the Ammonoosuc River at Woodsville in Grafton County, built in 1829, is the oldest existing Town lattice truss. Several miles upstream, the 1832 vintage Bath Village Bridge uses an interesting local variant of the Burr truss, featuring braces that overlap the panels of the truss, and solid integral arches. The Blair Bridge in Campton spans the Pemigewasset River with a Long truss that includes counterbrace wedges to prestress the truss, as the inventor recommended.

The White Mountain resorts of Carroll County have several covered bridges, all Paddleford trusses, although most of them have been heavily reworked. Cheshire and Sullivan counties, in the southwest, have several interesting bridges. Ashuelot Upper Village Bridge near Winchester is especially attractive, a white-painted Town lattice with outside sidewalks on both sides. Merrimack County

includes the nation's oldest covered railroad bridge at Contoocook, recently restored by master framers Arnold Graton and Tim Andrews for the National Society for the Preservation of Covered Bridges. Southern New Hampshire also has two boxed pony trusses, one on a public road in Wilton, and the other on a private farm lane in Rollinsford.

Maine always had fewer covered bridges than Vermont or New Hampshire, but the state still has seven old covered bridges, plus rebuilds of one bridge lost to arson, and of another to flood. Five of the bridges are Paddleford trusses in the western mountains region.

SOUTHERN NEW ENGLAND

Massachusetts has long followed a policy of replacing its relatively few old covered bridges with modern ones, sometimes fairly close copies, sometimes beefed up beyond recognition. By now the state has only two original covered bridges, both of them much reworked. However, a third was moved in from Vermont in 1952 and graces the museum collection at Old Sturbridge Village.

Connecticut still has two historical covered bridges over the Housatonic River in the northwest corner of the state. Hart's Bridge, at the lovely village of West Cornwall, is still in use on a numbered state highway. Bull's Bridge in Kent

Ashuelot Upper Village Bridge near Winchester is a popular landmark of southern New Hampshire. The Town lattice trusswork is clearly visible, but well protected by generous eaves that cover a sidewalk on each side.

The floor of Fitch's Bridge near East Delhi, New York once sloped up at one end to meet a steep grade. This unusual feature was later eliminated during repairs.

spans a scenic gorge. A third covered bridge, southeast of Hartford near East Hampton, was torn down in 2011 and replaced with a modern copy.

NEW YORK AND NEW JERSEY

The Catskill Mountains and surrounding territory are rich in covered bridges. Most famous is Perrine's Bridge, a Burr truss visible from the northbound lanes of the New York State Thruway at Rifton. However, the typical Catskills covered bridge is a Town lattice truss. Several show an interesting local variant with fan-shaped end bracing, intended to concentrate the load more specifically at the end points of the bridge. Three of the four covered bridges in Sullivan County share this style. Fitch's Bridge in Delaware County once did too, but it was reworked to a generic pattern during recent repairs.

New York's covered bridge gem is the Hyde Hall Bridge north of Cooperstown, spanning Shadow Brook on what was once a vast private estate. Dating from around 1825, it is the oldest existing covered bridge in North America. It is an early example of the Burr truss, and has been sensitively restored. New Jersey's last old covered bridge stands near Sergeantsville in Hunterdon County.

PENNSYLVANIA, DELAWARE, AND MARYLAND

Pennsylvania has 183 historical covered bridges, more than any other state, plus a small but increasing number of modern complete replacements. A laudable desire to keep the old bridges in service led to a major statewide restoration program beginning around 1990. Results have been mixed. Exterior appearance is carefully maintained unchanged, and some bridges on lightly traveled roads have been restored sensitively with most of the original framing intact. Many others have had their floor systems replaced with hidden steel beams. A few, notably the Pine Grove Bridge on the Chester–Lancaster county line, have been so denatured that they no longer seem historic.

Lancaster County has long been a destination for tourists seeking a taste of rural life, yet it is also home to over half a million people. The county has done well to retain twenty-six historical covered bridges, and there are also three recent rebuilds. Lancaster bridges are mostly Burr trusses with red-painted sides and white portals, and black diagonal warning stripes along the entry. Chester County is also experiencing much suburban pressure, but is still home to eleven historical covered bridges, plus two shared with Lancaster.

Philadelphia still has a covered bridge in the northern reaches of Fairmount Park. Bucks County, to the north, is home to ten old Town lattice trusses. In Pennsylvania the county governments were responsible for building covered bridges, not the towns as in New England, so the

Wenger's Mill Bridge was typical of the older appearance of covered bridges in Lancaster County, Pennsylvania. Here we see it during spring floods. It has since been re-housed in a more modern style.

covered bridge styles often vary by the county. Bucks also has a rare boxed pony truss in Ralph Stover State Park near Point Pleasant.

Stepped false-front portals of various styles were a specialty once found on many covered bridges of southeastern Pennsylvania, and occasionally further afield. Berks County has three covered bridges with false-front portals, and Chester, Lehigh, Franklin, and Montour counties have one each.

Columbia County has twenty-one old covered bridges, mostly either Burr trusses or queenposts. Formerly they were unpainted, and presented a very old-time look, but since the 1950s nearly all of them have been painted red.

Several central Pennsylvania counties have significant populations of covered bridges, notably Perry, Bedford, and Somerset, with joinery details and housing styles varying by the county. Cumberland and York counties were once rich in covered bridges too, but there the county commissioners systematically eliminated them in the middle of the twentieth century.

Pennsylvania's southwestern counties of Washington and Greene have many covered bridges of modest size hidden in

Crawford Bridge is an example of the modest but pretty covered bridges of Washington County, Pennsylvania.

pretty landscapes of steep hills. Here the simple kingpost and queenpost trusses are widely used. Most of the bridges were unpainted, but from the 1950s the Washington County commissioners decided to paint theirs red.

Maryland has six covered bridges, similar in appearance to those of adjacent parts of Pennsylvania, and Delaware has just one left.

THE SOUTH

Covered bridges are widely distributed south of the Mason–Dixon Line, although somewhat less profusely. They were common in the past from Virginia through Mississippi, but economic hard times meant that they received little maintenance. When funds did become available, replacement was the option usually chosen. Randolph County, North Carolina is a dramatic example of this trend. In 1937 it had forty-two covered bridges, but by 1955 only two were left.

Virginia has eight covered bridges, of which the most famous is the Humpback Bridge near Covington. It has a multiple-kingpost truss with radically arched chords

Carrollton Bridge has spanned Buckhannon River in Barbour County, West Virginia since the 1850s.

rising a little over four feet in the middle, so that the entire bridge appears to be leaping across Dunlap Creek. West Virginia's hilly landscape was once full of covered bridges. The best known today is the crossing of Tygart Valley River at Philippi, a rare double-barrel bridge still in service on US Route 250, although steel beams have carried the loads since the 1930s.

The Carolinas have just three old covered bridges between them. Georgia has eleven, mostly well-built Town lattice trusses. This style was favored by Horace King, a freed slave who went on to become one of the South's most successful covered bridge builders. Two of Georgia's existing covered bridges were built by his sons.

Alabama has eight covered bridges, and the Town lattice truss was popular here too. Several long, dramatic examples on tall slender piers grace the hilly landscape of Blount and Cullman counties. Tennessee is down to just three covered bridges, but the Doe River Bridge at downtown Elizabethton is of special interest because of its unusual hip roof.

Kentucky has eight old covered bridges, plus several controversial recent rebuilds. To the great credit of her informed citizens, Fleming County demanded a stop to the practice of replacing old covered bridges with modern copies, and instead received a beautiful, authentic restoration of the much-loved covered bridge at Goddard, supervised by Milton Graton's son Arnold.

Kilgore's Mill Bridge on the Barrow–Walton county line was typical of the well-built Town lattice trusses of Georgia. Sadly it fell into disrepair and was lost to arson in 1993.

OHIO

Ohio, with 112 old covered bridges, is second in number only to Pennsylvania, and has more variety in construction types than any other state. Here the older truss forms of multiple-kingpost, Burr, and Town lattice found a home alongside the more modern Howe and Smith trusses, with a selection of rarer types as well. The repair record varies by the county, but in Ohio bridges often emerge from renovation completely changed in appearance.

Since 1983 Ohio has also built a number of all-new covered bridges, mainly due to the enthusiasm of former Ashtabula County engineer John Smolen. After designing major reinforcements for several old covered bridges, he went on to build some all-new ones at sites that had not had covered bridges before. He even designed his own truss, a modification of an 1844 design by T. Willis Pratt, which was usually built in steel. At first the new bridges were of traditional proportions, but the more recent examples have been on well-traveled roads and could best be described as gigantic. They have no connection with historical covered bridges, but they demonstrate the appeal of the concept.

Trinity School Bridge in Lawrence County was one of Kentucky's youngest covered bridges, dating from 1924.

Although the lovely hill country of southeastern Ohio was once full of covered bridges, only Washington County still has any large numbers. The multiple-kingpost truss is popular in this part of the state, and some examples show a regional specialty in floor framing: the floor beams are suspended below the bottom chord of the truss by means of an iron strap that loops up around a large wooden peg straddling the chord timbers.

Central Ohio once had a covered-bridge lover's paradise in Fairfield County, which as recently as 1965 still had thirty-five of them. Today, only one recent rebuild remains in service. A few have been bypassed, and many others

Barkhurst Mill Bridge still stands amidst the southern Ohio hills in Morgan County. It fell into poor condition after this view was taken in 1976, and was scheduled for repairs in 2014.

Blacklick Bridge collapsed in 1977 after decades of neglect—a dramatic symbol of the decline of covered bridges in Fairfield County, Ohio.

have been given away and moved by public or private parties that wanted them. Union and Franklin counties have several examples of the rare Partridge truss, patented by local builder Reuben Partridge of Marysville. In western Ohio, Preble County has six examples of the equally rare Childs truss, and they have always been kept in good repair. Other western counties have a few covered bridges, including some Long trusses.

INDIANA

Indiana is tied with Vermont, having eighty-five historic covered bridges. Twenty-nine of these are in Parke County, where there are two recent rebuilds of bridges accidentally lost. The figures make this western Indiana county the American champion in covered bridge preservation. The secret has been consistent good maintenance; the prudent commissioners never neglected their bridges here. Nearly

Conley's Ford Bridge is one of the many attractions in America's top covered bridge county: Parke County, Indiana.

all are Burr trusses by local builders such as J. J. Daniels and J. A. Britton, and the last one was built in 1920.

Eastern Indiana, meanwhile, has some distinctive covered bridges built by three generations of the Kennedy family from Rushville. Their bridges are immaculately framed Burr trusses with graceful arched portals adorned with scrollwork and elaborate roof brackets; the sides are neatly clapboarded and painted white.

Metamora, in southeastern Indiana, is home to an unusual covered canal aqueduct. Visitors enjoy the strange impression of seeing water flow through the covered bridge, as well as under it. Other attractions in south-central Indiana include a 459-foot three-span Burr truss over the East Fork of the White River near Medora, and a 402-foot two-span Howe truss high over the same river near Williams, both by noted builder J. J. Daniels.

Smith Bridge in Rush County, Indiana is typical of the beautiful covered bridges built by the Kennedy family of nearby Rushville.

Duck Creek Aqueduct at Metamora, Indiana is the nation's last covered canal aqueduct. Such structures were never common.

ELSEWHERE IN THE MIDWEST

Illinois has a few examples of Howe and Burr trusses. Missouri has four covered bridges widely scattered across the state. Iowa has seven old bridges, plus one rebuild after arson. Most of these are in Madison County, where local builder H. P. Jones used roofs that are nearly flat. Michigan has three old covered bridges; Wisconsin and Minnesota have one each.

THE WEST COAST

California has ten covered bridges widely distributed throughout the northern half of the state. Knight's Ferry Bridge east of Oakdale is surely the most impressive, stretching 330 feet across Stanislaus River in the midst of the dry Sierra foothills. Bridgeport Bridge, over the South Fork of the Yuba River near North San Juan, has the longest clear span of any existing covered bridge, and measures 208 feet between the abutments.

Oregon still has forty-two historic covered bridges. All of the existing examples were built in the twentieth century, some as recently as the 1940s and early 1950s. Nearly all are Howe trusses. Lane County has the greatest concentration with sixteen. Here the bridges are usually painted white with the sides boarded high, and many have graceful, elliptically arched portals. Pengra Bridge near Jasper has the longest single sticks known to have been used for covered bridge chords, measuring 16 by 18 inches by 126 feet, all in one piece. Linn County, just to the north, paints its covered bridges white too, but prefers open sides. Meanwhile Lincoln County uses red paint, with flared siding that makes the bridges look like arrows pointing upwards. Douglas County has five covered bridges in a variety of housing styles; several other Oregon counties have a few covered bridges.

Washington has no old covered bridges left, and never officially encouraged their construction as did Oregon. Gray's River Bridge in Wahkiakum County is often cited with a 1905 date, but the existing bridge was really built in 1989. Eastern Washington has the interesting Harpole Bridge near Colfax, a former railroad bridge with sides

The unusual Cavitt Creek Bridge in Douglas County, Oregon was designed to permit the passage of log trucks.

boarded separately, and lateral bracing overhead, but no complete roof.

CANADA

Québec is a covered bridge paradise, with eighty-three historical covered bridges. The Eastern Townships region around Sherbrooke has a number of covered bridges from the nineteenth century, but elsewhere most of the existing bridges were built in the twentieth century by the Department of Colonization to facilitate settlement in new areas being opened for agriculture. With only a few exceptions, the province has resisted the temptation to add hidden steel beams, or to replace historical covered bridges with modern ones.

New Brunswick is home to sixty old covered bridges, and one rebuild of an old bridge destroyed by accident. The province once had some of the longest covered bridges in existence over its wide rivers and coastal estuaries. All of the long bridges are gone now except for the one at Hartland over the Saint John River, measuring 1,282 feet in seven spans. It is the longest covered bridge in the world.

This former bridge over the Memramcook River at Upper Dorchester, New Brunswick was the second longest covered bridge in the world at 848 feet.

Shepody River Mouth Bridge at Riverside-Albert had the hip roof once found on many New Brunswick covered bridges.

Most of New Brunswick's covered bridges are Howe trusses, but the province also has several examples of a regional variant of the Burr truss. Although many of the older covered bridges used a distinctive hip-roofed housing, only two examples remain. New Brunswick also built non-covered, creosoted-timber trusses in both the Howe and Burr styles, some of which remain in service.

The famed twin covered bridges at St. Martins, New Brunswick still span tidewater in this small fishing village, although sidewalks have been added to them since this view was taken in 1976.

GLOSSARY

Abutment The structure on the riverbank which supports the end of a bridge.

Bent A light framework made of a few upright posts with cross bracing, used occasionally to support a bridge in lieu of abutments, or as temporary reinforcement for an old bridge.

Brace A diagonal piece in a truss inclining inwards towards the center of the bridge, carrying loads in compression. See also counterbrace.

Chord The horizontal piece at the top or bottom of a truss frame, to which the posts or other pieces are attached.

Clear span The open space which is in fact spanned by a bridge, uninterrupted between the faces of the abutments or other supports. Clear span is distinguished from structure length, which also includes that part of the bridge resting on top of the abutments on land.

Counterbrace A diagonal piece in a truss inclining away from the center of the bridge. In the Long truss, wedges allow the counterbraces to be prestressed to a determined load, so that the bridge will not deflect in use.

Hip roof A roof having triangular ends sloping down directly to all four walls, without a gable. Hip roofs were rare on covered bridges, except in New Brunswick, Canada. The last hip-roofed covered bridge in the United States is at Elizabethton, Tennessee.

Mortise and tenon A joint in which a projecting tongue (the tenon) on the end of one timber fits into a corresponding pocket (the mortise) cut into the face of another timber, pinned with treenails.

Post A vertical piece in a truss, which in most designs functions in tension. Some trusses substituted metal rods for timber posts.

Treenail (pronounced trunnel, and occasionally spelled that way): A wooden peg which fits into a hole bored through a joint in order to secure it.

Truss A framework built up of small pieces arranged into a succession of rigid triangles, which can carry loads across spans much longer than the individual pieces themselves. The simplest trusses are the kingpost, with one post in the middle, and a brace on either side sloping down to the bottom chord; and the queenpost, which is similar but has two posts forming a box in the middle.

FURTHER READING

Allen, Richard Sanders, *Covered Bridges of the Northeast*, Stephen
   Greene Press, 1957 (most recently reprinted by Dover, 2004)
———, *Covered Bridges of the Middle Atlantic States*, Stephen
   Greene Press, 1959
Arbour, Gérald, and others, *Les Ponts Couverts au Québec*,
   Les Publications du Québec, 2005 (in French)
Burk, John S., *Massachusetts Covered Bridges*, Arcadia, 2010
Caswell, William S., Jr., *Connecticut and Rhode Island Covered Bridges*,
   Arcadia, 2011
Cockrell, Bill, *Oregon's Covered Bridges*, Arcadia, 2008
Conwill, Joseph D., *Maine's Covered Bridges*, Arcadia, 2003
———, *Vermont Covered Bridges*, Arcadia, 2004
———, *New England Covered Bridges through Time*, Fonthill, 2014
———, articles in *Timber Framing* on technical details of various
   trusses: Paddleford, March 2005; Burr, December 2005;
   Howe, September 2007; Long, March 2008; truss typology,
   December 2011
Jurgensen, Melissa C., and Laughlin, Robert W. M., *Kentucky's
   Covered Bridges*, Arcadia, 2007
Marshall, Richard G., *New Hampshire Covered Bridges*, New
   Hampshire Department of Transportation (NHDOT), 1994
Miller, Terry E., and Knapp, Ronald G., *America's Covered Bridges:
   Practical Crossings—Nostalgic Icons*, Tuttle, 2014
Moll, Fred J., *Pennsylvania's Covered Bridges*, Arcadia, 2012
Wilson, Richard R., *New York State's Covered Bridges*, Arcadia, 2004

Readers will also enjoy the detailed website on covered
bridge history maintained by William S. Caswell and Trish
Kane, *Covered Spans of Yesteryear*, at www.lostbridges.org.

INDEX